Roberto
CLEMENTE

CLEMENTE
nd Humanitarian

by Lew Freedman

ABDO
Publishing Company

Content Consultant: Mike Stadler PhD
Associate Professor of Psychology
University of Missouri

Published by ABDO Publishing Company, 8000 West 78th Street, Edina, Minnesota 55439. Copyright © 2011 by Abdo Consulting Group, Inc. International copyrights reserved in all countries. No part of this book may be reproduced in any form without written permission from the publisher. SportsZone™ is a trademark and logo of ABDO Publishing Company.

Printed in the United States of America,
North Mankato, Minnesota
112010
012011

 THIS BOOK CONTAINS AT LEAST 10% RECYCLED MATERIALS.

Editor: Chrös McDougall
Copy Editor: Paula Lewis
Series Design: Christa Schneider
Cover Production: Christa Schneider
Interior Production: Christa Schneider

Library of Congress Cataloging-in-Publication Data
Freedman, Lew.
  Roberto Clemente : baseball star & humanitarian / by Lew Freedman.
    p. cm. — (Legendary athletes)
  Includes bibliographical references and index.
  ISBN 978-1-61714-754-8
  1. Clemente, Roberto, 1934-1972. 2. Baseball players—Puerto Rico—Biography. 3. Generosity. I. Title.
  GV865.C45F74 2011
  796.357092—dc22
  [B]
                          2010041161

TABLE OF CONTENTS

Roberto Clemente was only four hits short of 3,000 for his career after getting his second hit against the Philadelphia Phillies on September 26, 1972.

Chasing 3,000 Hits

The suspense grew. As leaves began to fall from their trees at the end of September, announcing the coming autumn, the famous Pittsburgh Pirates outfielder had one item of unfinished business. Roberto Clemente was bombarded with phone calls and good luck wishes as the 1972 Major League Baseball season approached its end. He was approaching a number rarely obtained in pro baseball. At that time, only ten players in all of Major League Baseball history—dating back to 1876—had attained 3,000 career hits.

Any batter who accumulated a combination of 3,000 singles, doubles, triples, and home runs during his career was considered one of the greats in the game's history. As the eighteenth season of Clemente's career wound down, he was within a handful of hits of reaching that milestone and becoming a near-certain selection for the Baseball Hall of Fame. Gathering that many hits meant a ballplayer had proven himself over time and

The President Writes

After the 1972 season concluded, Clemente returned to his off-season home in Rio Piedras, Puerto Rico. He received an unexpected complimentary letter from Washington DC, written by President Richard M. Nixon. The president wrote:

"With the excitement of the playoffs and the World Series, I had neglected to tell you how delighted I was to learn of your 3,000th hit in major league ball. This new milestone is further confirmation—if any were needed—of the standards of excellence you have shown on the playing field. Heartiest congratulations and kindest good wishes for many more seasons."[1]

was worthy of such special recognition.

At the beginning of the 1972 season, Clemente was just 118 hits short of the benchmark number. If he played with his usual flair and capability, it seemed certain he would reach it that season. But he suffered injuries to his ankle and his heel that caused him to miss 47 of the Pirates' first 116 games. After that, he had only 39 games remaining to complete his quest for that year.

Clemente was a popular player not only in Pittsburgh but throughout the sport. That was especially true in Latin America. Born in Puerto Rico, Clemente was proud of his Hispanic heritage and was vocal about it. His first language was Spanish. Latino members of the baseball fraternity, regardless of what team they played on, looked up to him. Clemente was a role model for Latin Americans. He was particularly revered in Puerto Rico for his accomplishments on the field and for the generosity of his charity work.

Because he was so well known and so admired, most everyone in baseball wanted Clemente to record his 3,000th hit for the Pirates before the end of the '72 season. If not, he would have to wait until the new season began in April 1973 to reach that goal. People wanted Clemente to enjoy the milestone now, not spend months worrying about obtaining it.

Time's Running Out

Clemente thought much the same way. On September 27, 1972, with only a few days remaining in the season, he cracked two hits in a road game against the Philadelphia Phillies. That gave him 2,998

Doing the Right Thing

Former Pirates' manager Danny Murtaugh said Clemente always thought about things more significant to the world than baseball. "When he was approaching his 3,000th hit, I asked him if that would be the most important thing in his life. 'No, Danny,' he said, 'I have a project going in Puerto Rico for the underprivileged.'" Clemente was talking about his plans for a "Sports City" for youth in his home country.[2]

Lots of Hits at Once

Clemente earned his 3,000 major league hits in 9,454 at-bats while playing in 2,433 games. If 3,000 career hits is a prime measuring stick of a great hitter, a main seasonal yardstick for determining a top hitter is whether or not he gathers 200 hits in a season. Clemente did this four times.

for his career. A day later, he recorded one more hit. However, instead of trying for the special 3,000th hit in his next at-bat, Clemente requested that his manager, Bill Virdon, take him out of the game. The versatile, hard-hitting player had spent his entire career representing the people of Pittsburgh, Pennsylvania. Now he wanted to stroke that all-important hit at home, in his adopted city. He wanted to give the local fans a thrill.

On September 29, the Pirates opened a series against the New York Mets at their home park, Three Rivers Stadium. Tom Seaver, the most famous of Mets pitchers, was on the pitcher's mound. In his first at-bat that day, Clemente bounced a grounder up the middle of the diamond, past Seaver, and then it took a funny hop. New York's second baseman, Ken Boswell, reached out his glove, but did not grasp the baseball cleanly. He juggled the ball and Clemente was safe at first base. He appeared to have achieved his goal.

The crowd of more than 24,000 fans cheered. But they were to be disappointed. Clemente was safe at first base, but the official scorekeeper deemed that Boswell should have made the play. Therefore, an error was charged and Clemente's hit did not count on the stat sheet.

Over the years, Clemente had been outspoken. He was always bold enough to say what he thought. If he

No Sleep

In the weeks leading up to Clemente's 3,000th hit, he was under a lot of pressure. He wanted to finish the chase for the mark. But the harder he tried, the worse he did. He made more outs than hits and knew that with the Pirates' regular season ending soon, he might run out of time.

When he arrived at Three Rivers Stadium for the key game against the New York Mets, Clemente was frustrated. He was also very tired because he had not slept. He fielded telephone calls all night from friends and relatives in New York and Puerto Rico who shared his disappointment that his at-bat that night had been ruled an error instead of a hit.

Early in the morning of the big game, Clemente had to drive his wife Vera to the airport to meet her friends. Finally, as he prepared for what would become the memorable at-bat, Clemente allowed his teammate and fellow star Willie Stargell to pick out a bat for him to swing. Stargell handed Clemente a bat heavier than he normally used and said, "Go get it."[3] Clemente got his hit.

Another Record

Once Clemente belted his 3,000th hit, he hoped to rest for the National League playoffs by sitting out the Pirates' final three regular season games. However, a Pirates public relations man realized that if the outfielder played in one more game, Clemente would pass Hall of Famer Honus Wagner for the team record in appearances. Clemente said he would get the record the next season, but the official urged him not to wait. So on October 3, 1972, Clemente entered the game against the St. Louis Cardinals as a defensive replacement in right field. He did not even bat in the game.

felt he had been discriminated against because he did not speak English as well as a high school teacher or because he was of Latino heritage, he made his feelings known. That was one reason his fellow Hispanics adored him. He spoke for them. On this night, he felt he had been robbed of something rightfully his and expressed anger after the game. "All my life they have been stealing hits from me," Clemente said.[4]

Later he acknowledged that it would be best if the special hit was clean and with no controversy attached.

Success at Last

The next day, September 30, the Pirates again faced the Mets in an afternoon game. New York's rookie pitcher, Jon Matlack, was on the mound when Clemente stepped into the batter's box in the fourth

Clemente finally achieved his 3,000th hit against the
New York Mets on September 30, 1972.

inning. Matlack promptly got a strike on Clemente.
But the hitter won the duel on the next pitch, smacking
Matlack's pitch to deep left-center field. As the ball
skipped toward the fence at Three Rivers Stadium,
Clemente ran out a double.

The 13,117 fans in the stadium applauded and
roared Clemente's name during a standing ovation.
Elated, Clemente took off his helmet and waved it. He

had finally done it. He had 3,000 hits written next to his name in the record book.

After smashing the key hit, Clemente celebrated the achievement and soaked up the praise of his teammates, baseball experts, and Pirates' fans. It was a highlight of his career. "I dedicated the hit to the Pittsburgh fans and to the people in Puerto Rico," he said.[5] What no one could foresee was that because of impending tragedy, Roberto Clemente would never again stroke a hit for the Pirates.

Roberto Clemente, shown in 1961, was a popular player and also a role model to many Latin Americans during his 18 seasons in the major leagues.

CHAPTER 2

San Juan, shown in 2002, is the capital of Puerto Rico. Roberto Clemente was born and raised in nearby Carolina.

Early Life

S ome youngsters imagine they will grow up to be policemen or firemen. From the time Roberto Clemente was a little boy, he dreamed of becoming a professional baseball player beyond the boundaries of his native Puerto Rico, an island in the Caribbean Sea.

When he was five, Roberto spent most of his free time throwing a rubber ball around in his room and catching it on the rebound. He did this over and over again. Sometimes, he kept up this personal game of catch right through mealtime. His mother had to order him to put the ball down and come to the table with the rest of the family.

Roberto, born as Roberto Clemente Walker on August 18, 1934, was the youngest of seven children in the family of Melchor and Luisa Clemente. The Clementes lived in Carolina, approximately 7 miles (11.3 km) southeast of San Juan, in a large wooden house. The Clementes were not rich. His father worked as a sugar plantation manager; his mother was a laundress.

But she also made lunches for the workers on the plantation her husband oversaw. To do this additional work, she sometimes started her day at 1:00 a.m. The household thrived on hard work. The Clementes were lower middle class, not poverty stricken. The family always had clothes to wear and food on the table.

The family was strengthened and amused itself by sharing stories and jokes. Roberto always praised his parents. He said they taught him well and created a loving home environment. "I owe so much to my parents," he said. "They did so much for me. I never heard my father or mother raise their voices in our home. I never heard hate in my house."[1]

Baseball on His Mind

Once he mastered the tricky bounces of the rubber balls that he wore out in his own games, Roberto took to playing ball outdoors. He met up with other neighborhood children and played baseball even before he started public school. His introduction to the organized

Destiny

Roberto's mother, Luisa, indulged his baseball playing in the house and at the local playground, but once he started school she had grander ambitions for him. She wanted him to go to college and become an engineer. Through such a white-collar job, she felt, he would be able to help people. But when it was clear that Roberto was going to become a major league ballplayer, she put no pressure on him to change his goals. Looking back at his devotion to the sport from his youth on, she said, "Roberto was born to play baseball."[2]

sport came on a muddy field populated by trees. It was far from a perfect baseball diamond. Roberto did not surrender his rubber balls completely, however. He carried them around and kept squeezing them in his bare hands. The constant pressure built up strength in his fingers and wrists.

The family did not have an unlimited budget to provide Roberto with baseball equipment. When he was unable to use tennis balls, he manufactured his own baseballs by shaping old newspapers and magazines into round objects. They did not bounce very well, but the youngster could still play catch.

Learning Values

Roberto's father, Melchor, cared more about what his son would be like in the future than his success on a baseball diamond. The message was always clear that Roberto was expected to be truthful, honest, and good to people less fortunate than he was. Melchor was not knowledgeable about baseball, but he held strong views about right and wrong. "My father used to say, 'I want you to be a good man, I want you to work, and I want you to be a serious person,'" Roberto recalled. "I grew up with that in mind."[3]

Roberto's parents discouraged rash behavior. Quiet in dealing with friends and teachers, Roberto was quick to utter one word: "*Momentito.*" Wait a minute. He would not undertake an activity until he was good and ready and had thought it through. He said this word so often that those closest to Roberto gave him his first nickname. They called him "Momen," short for *momentito*, and made fun of his deliberate nature.[4] Melchor and Luisa did not raise a headstrong boy.

The work ethic was stressed in the Clemente home. When young Roberto requested that his dad buy him a bicycle, Melchor informed him he would have to raise the money himself. A man who lived in the neighborhood made Roberto a deal. If Roberto would carry a milk can the half mile (.8 km) from the store to the man's house each day, the man would pay him. However, Roberto's income was only in the pennies each month. It took many repetitions of that walk over three years for Roberto to earn enough to purchase the $27 bicycle.

Puerto Rico was a hotbed of baseball during the major leagues' off-season. It hosted a popular winter league. Long before they were welcome in the majors, black ballplayers from the original 48 states played throughout Latin America. Roberto gravitated to rooting for Carolina's closest professional team, the San Juan Senators. The team's standout outfielder, Monte Irvin, was his favorite player.

Early on, Irvin was a star only in Puerto Rico and

Potential at the Park

Early on, Roberto gained notice in local newspapers for playing baseball well. He kept a scrapbook of his exploits. Roberto was far from a top player when he joined the Santurce Crabbers, but his raw skills inspired compliments. James Buster "Buzz" Clarkson, the manager of the Crabbers, immediately recognized that Roberto was gifted. In turn, Roberto credited Clarkson for his help. "Buck Clarkson used to tell me I am as good as anybody in [the] big leagues," Roberto said years later.[5]

Baseball stars, such as New York Giants center fielder Willie Mays, came to Puerto Rico to play winter league baseball in the off-season.

Family Tragedy

Roberto was just a baby when his sister Ana Iris died at the age of five from a fire. The accident happened when gasoline spilled onto firewood on a cooking stove located just outside the door of the family home. The gasoline ignited into a strong blaze. The flame set Ana Iris' dress on fire. Luisa Clemente rushed her little girl to the hospital, but Ana Iris suffered burns over 90 percent of her body. Roberto never knew his sister, but later in life he imagined her by his side and said he felt her presence.

the Negro Leagues. He later became a star with the New York Giants in the National League after Jackie Robinson broke the color barrier with the Brooklyn Dodgers in 1947. Irvin eventually was elected to the National Baseball Hall of Fame.

"I idolized him," Roberto said of the hard-hitting Irvin. "I used to wait in front of the ballpark just for him to walk by so I could see him."[6]

The Santurce Crabbers shared the same stadium with the Senators, but Roberto's allegiance to the Senators was established between the ages of 11 and 15 because of Irvin's great talents. More than ever, though, Roberto loved this sport.

By 15, Roberto was an esteemed softball player. Softball is similar to baseball, except the ball is larger and pitchers use an underhand delivery. A year later, he played hardball for the Juncos Mules, making the shift from shortstop to the outfield. Roberto's sparkling talent was beginning to emerge. He was shy and did not often talk on the field. But he made plenty of noise with his bat and glove. He was skinny, but growing toward his adult height of 5 feet 11.

Going Pro

Of all the teams that might spot the budding skills of Roberto and reach out for him, it happened to be the Crabbers—the team Roberto spent several years rooting against. Owner Pedrin Zorrilla was known as the "Big Crab." When Zorrilla attended a Juncos Mules game in 1952, one player caught his eye. Over a period of a few innings, Roberto hit a line drive for a hit off the fence, made a beautiful slide

All-Around Athlete

In 1952, Roberto became fascinated with the Olympic Games. The summer Olympics were held in Helsinki, Finland, that year, around the time that Roberto was emerging as a high school track star. He competed in the 400-meter dash, the high jump, and the javelin throw. Roberto was so good in the javelin that he thought he had a chance to represent Puerto Rico in the next Olympics. But to do so, he would have to put aside his baseball ambitions. He chose baseball.

while running the bases, made a daring catch against the wall, and made a slingshot throw back to the infield. "That boy, I must have his name," Zorrilla said.[7]

Pretty soon he not only knew Roberto's name, but he had signed him to his first professional contract, paying $40 a week.

Monte Irvin was a star in the Negro Leagues and for the New York Giants. Roberto Clemente idolized Irvin while growing up.

CHAPTER 3

Brooklyn Dodgers scout Al Campanis wanted to sign Clemente when the player was 18 years old, but Clemente still had to finish high school.

Being Discovered

Clemente began his professional baseball career with the Santurce Crabbers while he was still in high school. He was just 18 years old when he signed with the team in the fall of 1952. One of his prized possessions was the new baseball glove that was part of his deal with the team.

Clemente was a very raw player, but the club recognized that he had the makings of a star. Just a month into his Santurce stay, the Brooklyn Dodgers conducted a tryout camp for the major league club nearby. Among 70 hopefuls, he ran, fielded, hit, and threw for the professional scouts.

Clemente attracted the most attention. He amazed scouts with his powerful throwing arm. Clemente was a center fielder at the time and when he threw to third base, the ball looked as though it had been shot out of a gun. It was a sneak preview of what Clemente would accomplish in the major leagues as a right fielder when he routinely threw out bold runners trying for an extra base.

Al Campanis was the Dodgers' chief scout at the time. After watching Clemente throw, Campanis said that he almost did not care if the player could do anything else. "If the sonofagun can hold a bat in his hands, I'm gonna sign this guy," Campanis said.[1]

Clemente smashed the ball all over the field. When Campanis filed his official scouting report for the Dodgers, it would have made any student proud—he gave Clemente all As.

Neither Clemente, nor his family, was ready to accept an offer from a team in the United States, however. He had to finish high school in Puerto Rico. Earning that diploma ranked highly in the priorities of Clemente's parents.

Life with the Crabbers

Clemente spent the following season playing for

Scouting Report

When the Brooklyn Dodgers' scout Al Campanis wrote out his report on Clemente he assigned him the following grades: Arm, A+; Accuracy, A; Fielding, A; Reactions A; Hitting, A; Power A+.

On another line it read, "Definite Prospect? yes." Campanis added the comment, "Will mature into big man."[2]

the Crabbers. Or more accurately, he spent most of a season watching the Crabbers from a first-rate seat in the dugout. Pedrin Zorrilla signed Clemente, but he insisted that his rookie players watch and learn. Manager Clarkson, who had appeared in 14 games for the Boston Braves in the majors, wanted to play Clemente more. But the boss said no and insisted that Clemente stay on the bench. Clarkson spent as much time cheering up Clemente as he did coaching him. "The main thing I had to do was to keep his spirits up," Clarkson said. "He didn't realize how good he was. . . .

Education in the Outfield

Up until the time Clemente joined the Santurce Crabbers, he was primarily a center fielder because he was able to cover more ground than the other players. Crabbers manager Buzz Clarkson had other high quality outfielders, however, so he stuck Clemente in right field. This maximized the chances to use Clemente's powerful right arm.

In professional baseball, the base runners were smarter and more capable than they were at the high school or amateur level. That meant it took a very strong and accurate arm for a fielder to throw runners out at second base and even more so at third base. Runners often challenged Clemente's arm, making him prove that he could get them out. Clemente did just that. After Clemente threw out a few of the daring runners, other runners stopped trying to gain an extra base. Clemente's mere presence became a defensive weapon for the Crabbers.

Clarkson served as Clemente's main teacher for two years as the young player added muscle to his body. "He had a few rough spots," Clarkson said. "But he never made the same mistake twice. He was baseball savvy and he listened."[3]

I told him he'd be as good as Willie Mays some day. And he was."[4]

Not only was Clemente inexperienced, but Santurce already had talented outfielders. It was not until the next winter, 1953–54, that Clemente got the chance to fill a regular spot for the Crabbers. Now approaching 20, Clemente was a more mature prospect. By earning a batting average of .288, major league scouts from many teams became aware of him.

If Clemente had come of age less than a decade earlier, no American teams would have been interested in him. With his dark skin color, Clemente would have been snubbed, ignored because of racial prejudice. Prior to 1947, when Jackie Robinson broke the color barrier with the Dodgers, no black players had suited up in the majors for more than half a century. Clemente

Two Years in Santurce

After being kept under wraps and told to listen and learn, Clemente was very anxious to play more in his second year with the Crabbers. Manager Buzz Clarkson was very much on Clemente's side. Even though some veterans with more experience complained, Clarkson made Clemente a frequent starter. He came to the plate 219 times and batted .288 during the winter of 1953–54. It was just enough action to start the stampede of interest in him by major league clubs.

Just like Jackie Robinson, *right*, Clemente signed with the Dodgers and was sent to the minor league Montreal Royals.

came along when the doors were being opened for black players and those in Latin American countries as well.

Wooed by the Dodgers

The Dodgers were first in line in recognizing Clemente's potential. But they were not alone. The New

Softball

Roberto Clemente graduated from the rubber ball in his house to softball before he joined the Juncos Mules for his first true baseball experience. Even the softball team was fairly sophisticated. The players of the Sello Rojo team represented a rice packaging company. Consistent with all of his other activities—throwing the javelin and making long throws from the outfield for Santurce—Clemente's number one glowing attribute in softball was showing off a powerful arm by throwing runners out at first base.

York Yankees, the New York Giants, the St. Louis Cardinals, and the Milwaukee Braves also expressed interest in signing the outfielder.

The Giants envisioned an outfield that included Willie Mays, Clemente's idol Monte Irvin, and Clemente. That would have been one of the greatest outfield trios of all time. However, the Dodgers outflanked their New York rivals. While the Giants talked, the Dodgers offered Clemente a contract for $5,000 a year and a $10,000 signing bonus.

A day after the Dodgers made their proposal, the Milwaukee Braves offered Clemente $27,500 to join their organization. It was tempting, but Clemente did not know anything about the Midwest. The Dodgers were highly regarded for winning National League pennants and for being good to black players.

Being aggressive in pursuing the top available black players brought the Dodgers good will in black communities across the country and in other baseball communities such as Puerto Rico. So Clemente chose the Brooklyn Dodgers, even though he would make less money. "Brooklyn was a famous team," Clemente said. "I wanted to play for the Dodgers."[5]

Although the money Clemente received was barely more than a third of what he would have been paid by the Braves, it was the most the Dodgers had offered a new player since signing Robinson in 1945. However, the size of the package played a significant role in shaping Clemente's major league career. While Roberto dreamed of playing for the Dodgers, a quirk in baseball rules at that time made that unlikely.

Sealing the Deal

When Clemente made up his mind that he wished to play for the Brooklyn Dodgers, he was under 21 years of age. So his father, Melchor, signed the contract, too. Also, the contract was technically with the Montreal Royals, the Dodgers' top minor league affiliate, not the National League team.

Ignorant of the policies that would determine his future, Clemente joined the Brooklyn Dodgers organization. He imagined that he would take his place at Ebbets Field in Brooklyn playing alongside Robinson, Duke Snider, and Pee Wee Reese with the Dodgers. But it would never happen.

Clemente dreamed of playing for the Brooklyn Dodgers at famous Ebbets Field.

Pittsburgh Pirates general manager Branch Rickey often bragged that he knew Clemente would be a superstar after he saw Clemente play in Puerto Rico in 1957.

Becoming a Pirate

The Brooklyn Dodgers created a dilemma by giving Clemente the $10,000 bonus. Without that payout, Clemente would not have signed with the Dodgers. But under the rules of big-league baseball at the time, any player who received a bonus of more than $4,000 had to remain on the major league roster for a year. If the player was sent to the minors, another team could claim him in a special draft.

This rule had been adopted in order to hold down the level of bonuses being paid for untried talent. In this case, it backfired on the Dodgers. Clemente was not ready for the majors. He needed more seasoning to flourish. If the Dodgers kept him on their 1954 roster, he would hardly ever play and would not develop. Since the Dodgers were in the National League pennant race every year, they did not want Clemente to take up roster space that might be needed for another player. The Dodgers were in a predicament.

A Dodger Mistake

Finally, the Brooklyn Dodgers made a fateful choice that changed the course of baseball history. The Dodgers sent Clemente to their top minor league team, the Montreal Royals, with instructions not to play him very often. The Dodgers hoped to "sneak" Clemente through a season in Montreal. The Dodgers took a gamble that other teams might believe the outfielder was injured or that he was not very good, after all.

This attempt to hide Clemente failed miserably. Branch Rickey, the general manager of the Pittsburgh Pirates, had formerly been the general manager of the Dodgers and knew his old team's tricks. Rickey had also hired a man who became famous as the top talent expert in Latin America. This scout, Howie Haak, was aware of Clemente's potential.

As soon as the Dodgers assigned Clemente to Montreal,

20–20 Hindsight

As a young player, Clemente was impatient. He was impatient to play more. He was impatient for success. He did not have the perspective to look at his situation objectively and realize he was lucky to be a 21-year-old young man playing in the major leagues. He knew he was a good baseball player, but he did not understand the finer points of the game. All athletes, regardless of their natural ability, must keep on learning more about their sport in order to improve their games.

After playing for the Pirates for nearly a decade, Clemente recognized the type of player he had been as a rookie. "I wasn't ready for the majors when I joined the Pirates in 1955," he said. "I was too young and didn't know my way around."[1]

the Pirates took note. Doing their best to keep Clemente out of the limelight, the Royals used him in just 87 games during the 1954 season. Any time Clemente got hot, the Royals benched him, which frustrated the player. "When he was having a good day at Montreal, they'd yank him," said Clemente's old Santurce manager Buzz Clarkson.[2]

Clemente came to the plate only 148 times and batted just .257. He was benched for the season's last 25 games. Clemente had not understood that the Dodgers were handling him in a unique way because of

Prejudice

During the 1950s, nearly 100 years after the end of the American Civil War that concluded with black slaves being set free, American society still had not come to terms with relationships between its black and white citizens. The law read one way, but closed minds ruled in many parts of the country. As Clemente, with his dark skin and accented English, made his way in an unfamiliar land, the beginnings of the modern civil rights movement stirred.

Most Major League Baseball teams held spring training in Florida. Young black players faced discrimination in their daily actions and were assigned to stay in black areas of communities, apart from their white teammates.

In 1955, the Pirates met the Baltimore Orioles in an exhibition game in Birmingham, Alabama. Clemente was one of three Pittsburgh players forced to sit out the game and remain in street clothes because of a city law banning blacks and whites from playing on the same field. In 1956, the Pirates were scheduled for another exhibition in Birmingham, this time against the Kansas City Athletics, but the game was moved to New Orleans, Louisiana.

his bonus. He was so upset that he announced he was going to return to Puerto Rico.

When it became clear that Clemente was available because he was a "bonus baby," Pittsburgh snapped him up in the November 22, 1954, baseball draft. Clemente counted his experience in Montreal as a lost year, so he was excited when the Pirates drafted him and told him he was definitely going to be in the majors in 1955.

Clemente, who had long dreamed of playing for the Dodgers, became a Pirate. The Pirates paid Brooklyn just $4,000 to acquire a future Hall of Famer. The Pirates had to keep Clemente in the major leagues or they would risk losing him by making the same mistake the Dodgers did.

A Chance to Play

By 1955, when he turned 21, Clemente was a major leaguer. He played in 124 games as a rookie and batted .255. There were some rough times. At spring training in Florida, Clemente found out the Pirates' black players were not welcome in many of the business establishments. They could not sleep in the same hotels as their white teammates or eat dinner in the same restaurants. He was very disturbed by this injustice in American society.

Clemente was taken aback, as well, when sportswriters and other fans began referring to him as

Clemente made a diving catch during a 1956 game against the
Brooklyn Dodgers.

Bob for short. He was Roberto and was always going to
be Roberto. Also, Clemente spoke limited English. His
first manager, Fred Haney, did not speak Spanish, so
Roberto sometimes had difficulty communicating his
thoughts.

The Pittsburgh Pirates of the early 1950s were one
of the worst teams in baseball history. Finishing last
in 1954 enabled the team to draft and keep Clemente
while waiting for him to develop.

Temper, Temper

Clemente was still somewhat immature when he broke into the Pirates' lineup in 1955. If things did not always go his way, he exploded, often throwing tantrums in front of his teammates. If he made an out when he thought he should have made a hit, he sometimes destroyed Pirates team equipment.

The first time Clemente caused a scene, his surprised manager, Fred Haney, fined him $25. That did not cure Clemente's habit. Clemente had a tendency of throwing his batting helmet onto the ground after striking out. He broke 22 helmets that year. When informed that he would be sent a bill for $220, Clemente decided he had to improve his behavior. He could not afford the cost of giving into his temper.

While Clemente saw much more action as a rookie than he had in the minors, he didn't begin as a starter for the Pirates. A spectator at the start of the season, he waited for his chance to show his stuff. Eventually, he had that opportunity. The more he played, the better Clemente became. He displayed his promise in spurts, sometimes having a good hitting game and sometimes making a spectacular play in the outfield.

Clemente played well enough to justify the Pirates' decision to obtain him. But young Clemente was a nervous newcomer. "I was so afraid of making a mistake in right field that I had tunnel vision," he said. "I would concentrate so much on the hitter, I never even saw the pitcher, first or second baseman between me and the hitter."[3]

It was not long, however, before Clemente saw everything that happened on the baseball field very clearly.

Soon after joining the Pittsburgh Pirates, Roberto Clemente established himself as one of baseball's all-time greats.

From left to right, Roberto Clemente, Dale Long, Ken Boyer, and Rip Repulski led the National League in batting average through June 11, 1956.

Becoming a Star

By today's standards of the muscular athlete, Clemente was not a big man. As he reached adulthood, he was 5 foot 11 and his official weight was listed on team rosters as 175 pounds. But he always played larger.

After his rookie year, Clemente improved steadily. He emerged as one of the best young players in the National League. His batting average increased. His ability to drive in runs increased. And his fielding, always above average, continued to advance. Frequently, Clemente caught fly balls to right field in what was called a basket catch. Rather than following the normal form of raising his glove in the air and holding his other hand behind it to steady the mitt, he held his glove out in front of his belly, pocket up, and let the descending ball fall into it. Only Willie Mays had done this before with much success. Critics felt Clemente might be showing off unnecessarily. He said he was simply most comfortable catching the ball this way. As long as he did not drop it, why

Casual Racism

As a black man in a country with a white majority and as a black player in a sport with a white majority, Clemente was sensitive to slights. Some of those came from otherwise friendly newspapermen who thought they were complimenting Clemente, but offended him with their language. One such example was printed in a Pittsburgh newspaper: "The dusky Puerto Rican . . . played his position well and ran the bases like a scared rabbit. It seemed that every time we looked up there was Roberto showing his flashing heels and gleaming white teeth to the loud screams of the bleacher fans."[2]

should anybody care? He didn't drop many.

Clemente said Mays did not influence him. When he was in the Dodgers' system in 1954, Clemente changed styles at the urging of coach Herman Franks and Luis Olmo, a veteran player. "Before that I missed fly balls many times because I tried to catch them too high," Clemente said. "But I never dropped one ball since I used the basket catch."[1]

Breaking the .300 Barrier

In 1956, Clemente batted .311. Throughout his 18-season career, Clemente batted .300 or more 13 times. Never a huge power hitter, he drove in 60 runs in his 147 games. Still, throughout his first few years with the Pirates in the 1950s, the team and its young player were still trying to establish themselves at the top level of the sport.

Clemente and the Pirates suffered the growing pains together. The team tried to piece together a pennant contender by acquiring new pitchers and bringing up young players from the minors. Clemente worked hard on his hitting, his adaptation to American culture, and his knowledge of baseball. He discovered that it was good to possess great talent, but that a player had to concentrate and sweat to apply his natural ability to the circumstances faced in games.

Once Clemente hit .300 for the first time, sportswriters understood why he was so heavily promoted by management. In the *Pittsburgh Press*, Clemente was called "one of the most promising young athletes in the National League today" and "a once-in-a-lifetime ballplayer."[3] Soon, his number 21 jersey was

Maturing

After Clemente became a perennial All-Star, he was known as "the Great One," a great compliment to his ability and attitude. But in the 1950s, he was seen more as a ballplayer struggling to grow into his talent.

Frank Thomas shared the Pirates outfield with Clemente for four seasons between 1955 and 1958 and watched him start to grow up in the field and in the clubhouse while they were teammates. "He played his position well," Thomas said.

"He was a master at what he did." Thomas added, "He always liked kids. I had one long conversation with him, and he told me what he wanted to do in Puerto Rico. He had this dream to build a special Sports City for the kids, especially the poor kids. . . .

"I think he was genuine in his thinking. He cared for people. But like I say, I only spent four years with him when he wasn't really into his own yet. He was a young kid trying to make a name for himself."[4]

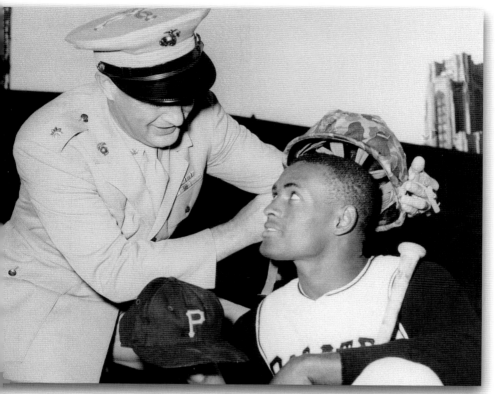

Maj. Luther Reedy gave Clemente a combat helmet after Clemente was sworn into the Marine Corps in 1958.

readily identifiable to Pirates fans. But not everything went smoothly for Clemente.

Injury Problems

Clemente experienced some great frustrations in his early twenties. For the first time, his athletic body experienced an injury that slowed him down in the field. He suffered from a back ailment in 1954 that was generated by an automobile accident. When Clemente was visiting Puerto Rico, a drunk driver shot through a red light and hit his car at 60 miles per hour (97 km/h). Some days, he could not stand up straight without extra effort. Other days, he could not run freely without pain.

Worse, because it was not an injury that required wearing a cast or bandage, some people did not believe that Clemente was really injured. He was disappointed to hear hints that he might be faking an injury and angrily denied those rumors. Other minor nagging woes such as stomach distress, headaches, or bone chips in his elbow kept Clemente out of the lineup too. He missed 43 games in 1957 and 50 games in 1959.

Much later, Clemente revealed to sportswriters that his mother and father wanted him to quit playing baseball in 1956 because of his back trouble. He said he briefly considered retirement when he could hardly suit up for his winter ball team in Puerto Rico.

Breakthrough

Things changed for Clemente in a major way in 1960. Although the back problem flared up periodically

Off the Field

Clemente liked to return to Puerto Rico to play winter ball. He enjoyed playing baseball in front of friends and family and considered it an obligation to perform for his longtime fans. However, Clemente could not return to his old Santurce team during the 1958–59 season. Instead, he served in the United States Marine Corps Reserves. For six months, he split his time between Parris Island, South Carolina, and Camp LeJeune in North Carolina.

for the rest of his life, Clemente felt healthy that season. At 26, he was entering his prime playing years and began showing his true potential. That year he batted .314, his second season above .300. He also helped lead the Pirates to their first World Series in 33 years. He was voted onto the National League All-Star team for the first time—the first of 12 selections. He was on his way.

Not only did Clemente hit over .300 in 1960, his statistics illustrated that he could do many things well. That year he hit 16 home runs with 94 runs batted in and scored 89 runs. He played superb defense and was a leader on the pennant-winning team. Clemente believed he should have won the National League's Most Valuable Player (MVP) award. He was crushed when he did not. "I had [my] best year in the majors and I was the league's most valuable player," he claimed, "but I didn't get one first-place vote."[5]

Clemente felt that disappointment deep in his heart. But the experience only made him work harder.

Trying to Get It Right

By 1960, it was obvious to those who got to know Clemente in Pittsburgh that he was a perfectionist. If he did not feel well, he said so. If he did not think things were going right with the team, he said so. If he thought umpires made a mistake, he said so. Gradually, it dawned on people that Clemente was outspoken about baseball matters because he wanted to win so badly. But he did not simply blame mistakes on others. He was hard on himself. "I am always mad at myself," Clemente said.[6]

In 1960, Clemente, *right*, and San Francisco Giants outfielder Willie Mays, *left*, battled for the National League batting title. Mays ended up third and Clemente was fourth.

Roberto Clemente sat with family members during the 1970 season. *From left to right*, mother Luisa, son Roberto Jr., Clemente, sons Luis and Richie, and wife Vera.

Hispanic Pride

Clemente's parents raised him to be proud of his home, his family, his Hispanic heritage, and of himself. He took their lessons to heart. Clemente carried himself with his shoulders thrown back, standing tall. He looked people in the eye when he talked with them.

What he hated, though—what infuriated him—was when sportswriters quoted his English words the way they sounded to them rather than what he intended them to sound like. He felt many of the sportswriters of the 1950s and 1960s tried to make him sound dumb to the public by quoting him phonetically. Many sportswriters fix small errors in quotes if the edits do not change the meaning of the quote.

Clemente felt that the writers he encountered with the Pirates were nationalistic to a fault. He felt that the only thing that mattered to them about a man was that he spoke "good" English, looked like them (meaning white), and came from the United States. To those writers, Clemente

Political Spokesman

It was not only Latin American players who gained respect for Clemente when he spoke out against what he thought were discriminatory practices. Black American ballplayers had suffered many of the same types of slights, so they cheered on Clemente's campaign to earn more dignity for Latinos. "All the Latins wanted was some respect," said Monte Irvin, a Clemente contemporary and Hall of Famer who is black, "and Clemente was responsible."[1]

believed, he was an alien because he grew up in Puerto Rico. Even though Puerto Rico was a territorial possession of the United States, and he was a citizen with the same rights, Clemente thought the writers— and many others—classified him as an outsider.

Latino Spokesman

Clemente saw himself as a representative of Puerto Rico. As he matured and aged, he understood that he was a powerful symbol for other Latino ballplayers and for the youth of Puerto Rico and other Latin American countries. They admired him not only for his achievements on the baseball diamond, but because he could be a role model.

For much of his career, Clemente believed sportswriters misunderstood him. He felt that they held it against him that he was black and Hispanic. He also thought they disapproved of him because he said whatever was on his mind and did not go out of his way to make friends with them. "I do not kiss the writers' boots," Clemente said, adding that he was attacked in newspapers as a lazy player and accused of faking injuries, "because I am black and because I am a foreigner."[2]

Jackie Robinson integrated twentieth-century Major League Baseball only eight years before Clemente debuted on the Pirates' roster. The United States in the 1950s was beginning a period of tremendous upheaval when blacks took to the streets to march and demonstrate for equality. Clemente believed that the

Insults in His Own Words

Perhaps the thing that Clemente hated the most in his dealings with the sportswriters who wrote about the Pittsburgh Pirates was the way they made him sound. Reporters would ask questions. Clemente would answer. He told them what he was thinking. But because he was quoted directly in his accented English, Clemente felt he was being made out to sound stupid. That angered him. He believed his message got lost in the translation of broken English to English.

One example of the type of quoting that angered Clemente appeared in a *Pittsburgh Press* sports story during the 1955 season. Clemente was quoted as saying: "I no play so gut yet. Me like hot weather, veree hot. I no run fast cold weather. No get warm in cold. No get warm, no play gut. You see."[3] Clemente was likely trying to say: "I don't play so good yet. I like hot weather, very hot. I do not run fast in cold weather. I don't get warm in the cold. If I don't get warm, I don't play good. You see?"

When such reports showed up in the newspapers, Clemente felt betrayed. To him he was purposely being made out to be a fool. During Clemente's playing career there were almost no Spanish-speaking reporters.

arrival of black-skinned Latinos in baseball touched off a different form of prejudice against him and other Hispanics. "Because they speak Spanish among themselves," Clemente said of Latino players, "they are set off as a minority within a minority, and they bear the brunt of the sport's remaining racial barriers."[4]

Other Latin American ballplayers nodded their heads in agreement when Clemente spoke up. He was speaking for them, too, telling the baseball world that it was hard to be both black and Hispanic and succeed in a difficult sport while trying to adapt to a new culture. "We need somebody to speak for us, but not just to talk," said Aurelio Rodriguez, a 17-year major league player from Mexico. "The thing about Clemente is that he had something to say."[5]

When Clemente was not quoted in broken English, he sounded very articulate. He clearly gave a great deal of thought to his answers. They revealed his strong feelings and made it obvious that he thought about many important issues beyond baseball.

Another Side of Clemente

When Clemente arrived at the ballpark to play a game for the Pittsburgh Pirates, he was all business. The park was his office. He had a serious game face. But when he was away from the park, among friends, and usually speaking Spanish, Clemente showed off a different personality. He cracked jokes and bantered with those closest to him. "He was very light, spiritually speaking, among friends," said Luis Mayoral, a longtime friend. "There was a peaceful Roberto Clemente, a funny Roberto Clemente."[6]

Clemente was a role model for many, especially youngsters.

Giving Kids Hope

Clemente's success on the field made him famous. When he visited Puerto Rico, he watched the way people responded to him as a star ballplayer, especially youngsters. He saw so much sadness and poverty among the children. Clemente wanted to inspire hopes and dreams in the younger generation. For years, he visited neighborhoods in distressed areas to talk about how to follow a good path in life.

Clemente began planning a way to use sports to help youthful Puerto Ricans stay away from drug use, gain confidence, and perhaps even become professional athletes. He announced that it was his dream to found a "Sports City."

Late in his career, Clemente began working with businessmen to obtain federal grants and to raise funds to create the "city" that would provide classroom learning and athletic instruction.

Clemente understood that he had gained status in the eyes of the world because he was an All-Star baseball player. But he felt an obligation to those less fortunate, especially people with the same type of Latin American roots he had. Those feelings stemmed from his determination to be treated with dignity at all times. He once said, "This is something that from the first day, I said to myself: 'I am the minority group. I am from the poor people. I represent the poor people. I represent the common people of America. So I am going to be treated as a human being.'"[7]

Seeing the Future

Manny Sanguillen, a catcher for the Pirates, remembers riding in a taxi to the ballpark with Clemente for a World Series game against the Baltimore Orioles in 1971. Mike Cuellar was pitching for the Orioles that night. Clemente predicted that Cuellar was going to throw a very high, inside pitch to scare him in his first at-bat. Then, Clemente said, he would get up and hit the ball to the left portion of center field. Cuellar indeed did brush Clemente back from his usual spot in the batter's box, but Clemente improved on his prediction, smashing a home run out of the park.

While starring on the baseball diamond, Clemente dreamed of building a Sports City for poverty-stricken youth in Puerto Rico.

CHAPTER 7

The Pirates—and their fans—rushed onto the field when Bill Mazeroski hit a ninth-inning homer to win the 1960 World Series.

The Biggest Stage

Clemente's true breakthrough as a baseball star occurred in 1960. His fame only spread as the Pittsburgh Pirates won their first pennant in 33 years and then won one of the most dramatic World Series in history. The Pirates defeated the New York Yankees four games to three in the World Series. They won the championship when Bill Mazeroski hit the winning home run in the ninth inning of Game 7. The Pirates' accomplishments of 1960 remain some of the most cherished Pittsburgh sports memories.

The Pirates were an exceptionally good team that year. Clemente, already one of the key players, took on a larger role than ever. Winning a title provided great satisfaction to Clemente and playing in the nationally televised World Series introduced his talents to more baseball fans. Other than rare exceptions on game-of-the-week appearances, sports teams were only shown on TV in their hometowns.

A Hitting Machine

Clemente emerged as one of the best and most consistent hitters in baseball starting in 1960. He hit .314 that season—his second season above .300—and batted over .311 12 times during his last 13 seasons. He won his first batting title when he hit .351 in 1961. His career-best came in 1967 when he batted .357 to win his fourth batting title in seven years. Clemente also recorded three seasons where he had on-base percentages of more than .400. In 1969, he led the National League with 12 triples.

The Improved Model

Clemente's achievements that season marked a dividing line in his career. During the second half of the 1950s, Clemente steadily improved. Beginning in 1960, he was recognized as one of the best players in the sport.

All of Clemente's talents were on display in the 1960 World Series. He had at least one hit in every game, batting .310 in the Series. His great speed allowed him to cover large areas in right field. When the Pirates won, Clemente did not linger in the winning locker room for long. Some people later criticized him for not hanging around with his teammates. But he said he left Forbes Field and went to nearby Schlenley Park, where Pirates supporters were dancing in the streets. "We hugged each other," Clemente said. "I felt good being with them."[1]

After the 1960 World Series title, Clemente was on the map. In 1961, he hit .351 and won his first of four batting titles. He batted higher than .300 for eight years in a row including that important 1960 season

Clemente prepared to swing against the Chicago Cubs in 1965.
He won the league's batting title that year.

and made the National League All-Star team in every
one of those years. He won the league batting title in
1964, 1965, and 1967. Clemente also led the league in
hits twice.

"I knew he was good when we won the World Series
in '60," said Pirates pitcher Roy Face, "but I didn't know
he was going to have the career he ended up having.
He could do anything. He could hit, he could hit with

Aches and Pains

Throughout his career, Clemente complained of a number of physical ailments. When one sportswriter took the trouble to total them up, it seemed impossible that Clemente could have had so much wrong with him and still function at such a high level on the baseball field. At various times, Clemente said he had problems with disks in his back, headaches, stomach aches, bone chips in his elbow, a pulled muscle in his shoulder, repeated colds, a pulled muscle in his calf, stitches in his chin, a tonsillectomy, insomnia, and nightmares. Some believed he was a hypochondriac, complaining about imaginary illnesses.

power, he could run, he could field, and he could throw with the best of them."[2]

Each winter, Clemente went home to Puerto Rico. In 1960, because of the World Series, he did not return until late in October. His popularity attracted many new fans. He became even more popular among the old fans who already knew him well. The newspapers in San Juan reported his every move during the World Series and ran pictures of him every day. When Clemente's plane landed, it was greeted by hundreds of fans holding up welcome signs.

Love from Everywhere

Clemente was the guest of honor on his home island. Luncheons, dinners, and parties requiring his attendance continued for a month. The *San Juan Star* presented Clemente with a trophy stating he was the best Latin American player in the majors. His popularity in Latin America was at an all-time high.

By the 1960s, Clemente candidly said how he felt about his ranking in the sport. "For me, I am the best," he said.³ Some people did not react to that comment very well. They thought Clemente was too full of himself. Teammate Manny Sanguillen, a player from Panama, said Clemente was misunderstood on this count. "Some people thought he was bragging," Sanguillen said, "but that expression is an old Spanish saying that means, 'I did the best I am capable of doing.'"⁴

Latino Admiration

Chicago White Sox manager Ozzie Guillen, the first Hispanic manager to win a World Series, said Clemente was an important figure in the history of baseball for more than his on-field accomplishments.

"For me he is the Jackie Robinson of Latin baseball," said Guillen, who is from Venezuela. "He lived racism. He was a man who was happy to be not only Puerto Rican, but Latin American. He let people know that. And that is something that is very important for all of us."⁵

Likewise, Manny Mota, the longtime outfielder and Los Angeles Dodgers coach from the Dominican Republic, said Clemente was a man who was recognized for his role standing up for all Latino players during an era when having dark skin and speaking with an accent was often a target for prejudice. "He was a great person, a good human being, a person who would defend minorities," Mota said. "He was a leader and controversial because he didn't permit injustices in regards to race. He was very vocal, and that was difficult. He was very misunderstood. But he would not accept injustices with Latins nor with players of color. He was always there to defend them."⁶

But Clemente really did think he was the best. If he did not receive the number of votes he felt he should have for various honors, he spoke up, indicating that he thought he was more deserving than the winner. Part of this was Clemente's fierce pride. Part of this was to motivate himself. Clemente often played at his best when he was angry.

In his late twenties and early thirties, Clemente led the Pirates with his all-around skills from spring training until the end of the regular season. "I thought Roberto was the greatest player I've ever seen," said Clemente's longtime manager Danny Murtaugh. "He's a man who'll be remembered as long as baseball is played."[7]

Clemente had tremendous abilities. He could lash line drives to every corner of the ballpark and cruise around the bases with his long-legged strides. His powerful throwing arm scared base runners. He even caught the fly balls with style. Soon, other players were excited just to watch Clemente in action.

"He was the one player that players on other teams didn't want to miss," said Pirates' pitcher Steve Blass. "They'd run out of the clubhouse to watch him take batting practice. He could make a 10-year veteran act like a 10-year-old kid."[8]

Clemente, *right*, posed with National League president Warren Giles after Clemente was presented with a silver bat as the 1965 National League batting champion.

CHAPTER 8

Clemente won 12 Gold Glove Awards in the 1960s and early 1970s. The Gold Glove Award is given to the best fielder at each position.

The Great One

Once he became recognized as one of baseball's great stars, Clemente built upon his reputation. Year after year, he continued hitting over .300 and leading his Pittsburgh Pirates in every way possible. One of those was with his defense.

The Gold Glove Award is given to the best fielders at each position. During the 1960s and into the early 1970s, Clemente won 12 straight Gold Glove Awards for his play in the outfield. Clemente faced bigger challenges than most other right fielders because his home ballpark, Forbes Field, was more spacious than many other fields. He had to cover more ground than most right fielders.

"He was so graceful," said Branch Rickey III, whose grandfather was the general manager of the Pirates when they drafted Clemente. "Defensively, I don't expect to see another Clemente in my lifetime. That arm doesn't exist in the sport today."[1]

Clemente's fielding ability and strong arm were gifts, but he worked hard to develop them. His parents had taught him to work hard, and he applied that advice throughout his life.

In the years after the Pirates won the 1960 World Series, Clemente's talent for hitting a ball caught up to his self-image. By hitting .351 in 1961, Clemente clinched the idea for most baseball experts that he could hit as well as anyone.

"I believe I can hit with anybody in baseball," Clemente said. "Maybe I can't hit with the power of a

Family Ties

Clemente was a young, single man when he reached the majors with the Pirates in 1955. But the girl of his dreams—Vera Christina Zabala—was back in Puerto Rico. She and Clemente married in November 1964 when the baseball player was 30. They spent their honeymoon in the Virgin Islands.

Despite his fame in Puerto Rico and the United States, Clemente spent much of his free time away from baseball at home. Rather than attend parties, he preferred the company of his family. He fathered three sons, Roberto Jr., Luis Roberto, and Enrique Roberto.

The family's primary residence was in Puerto Rico. Although his children were old enough to see him play for the Pirates, they were not old enough to understand Clemente's status in the sport. They may have only sensed he was a famous man when a steady stream of visitors came to their home to see their father in Rio Piedras during the off-season.

Roberto Jr., the oldest, missed his father keenly whenever he left for baseball or other overnight business. Roberto Jr. would even hide his father's plane tickets in an effort to get Clemente to stay home.

Clemente married Vera Christina Zabala in November 1964 in Puerto Rico.

[Willie] Mays or a Frank Robinson or a Hank Aaron, but I can hit."[2]

Whether baseball people agreed with Clemente on his self-appraisal or not, Clemente felt compelled to make statements such as those because he believed the voters underestimated him when voting for awards. That changed when he started winning his dozen Gold Gloves and earning his dozen All-Star game selections.

Most Valuable Player

Whether the voters were biased or not, they could not ignore Clemente's 1966 season. Clemente played

Power When Needed

A very smart player, Clemente did not try to hit home runs very often for the Pirates. This was especially true at home in Forbes Field because the park was bigger than most. If he went for home runs, Clemente would likely have to sacrifice his .300 batting average. However, twice in his career he slammed three home runs in a game. The first time was in May 1967 against the Cincinnati Reds. The second time was in August 1969 against the San Francisco Giants.

in all 154 games for the Pirates that season. He smashed his career high of 29 home runs and collected his career high of 119 runs batted in. He also stroked 202 hits and batted .317. For that, he was named the MVP of the National League. He also won his sixth straight Gold Glove.

"I think he was the MVP because he did so many little things, things that some stars don't do," said Pirates manager Harry Walker, "hustling on routine ground balls, breaking up double plays, and hustling to take an extra base. By doing this, he set an example that others followed."[3]

The recognition as MVP made Clemente happy because it seemed to prove his case that he was the best. This was the mid-1960s and Clemente was at the peak of his baseball career. He could do everything asked of him on the field. One year after he took home the MVP trophy, he led the National League in hitting for a fourth time with a .357 average.

A Special Party

By 1970, Clemente had been a member of the Pirates for 15 years. It was clear that he was one of the best players in the history of the team. So Pittsburgh management honored him in a special way. On July 24, 1970, the Pirates declared "Roberto Clemente Night" at their new Three Rivers Stadium.

The special program from that night's events celebrated Clemente's career in many ways. It contained a brief biography of his playing career, a chart with his year-by-year playing statistics, comments from teammates and opponents, and a message to Clemente written in a format similar to a newspaper editorial. In part it read, "We thank you for the thrills you have given us—the clutch line drive, the sliding catch, the spectacular throw, and the extra base you dared to take. Pittsburgh is proud you are a Pirate."[4]

Clemente would not admit that he cried that night, but said he might have.

Manager Clemente

Clemente loved playing winter ball in Puerto Rico. His fans at home demanded it, and he felt he should play as long as he was able. But sometimes after the regular season, Clemente returned home from the Pirates with aches and pains that needed rest and recuperation. Playing additional games in the off-season might jeopardize his career. Near the end of his stay with the Pirates, however, Clemente came up with a solution that made everyone happy. He became the manager of a San Juan team. That kept him in the public eye and allowed his injuries to heal.

A Health Worry

The night before the 1971 World Series began between the Pittsburgh Pirates and the Baltimore Orioles, Clemente did not appear to be a player on the verge of his crowning moment in baseball. He was too sick to stand up. He had food poisoning and was so ill that his wife, Vera, thought he was going to be too weak to even play in the opening game. Usually open about his ailments, Clemente told few people he was sick that day, and then had two hits for the Pirates.

Another Series Win

Clemente was not finished providing thrills for Pittsburgh baseball fans. In 1971, after an absence of 11 years, the Pirates returned to the World Series. Despite injuries that limited Clemente to 132 games, he still batted .341.

The Pirates upset the favored Cincinnati Reds in the National League playoffs and then defeated the Baltimore Orioles to win the World Series again. This time, the most coveted individual award went to Clemente, who batted .414 in the Series. He was voted MVP, one of the highlights of his career. "Now," he said at the presentation ceremony, "everyone knows the way Roberto Clemente plays. I believe I am the best player in baseball today."[5]

Clemente rounded third base after hitting a home run in Game 7 of the 1971 World Series. Clemente was named MVP of that World Series.

CHAPTER 9

Among the highlights of the early 1970s for Clemente was being named Most Valuable Player of the 1971 World Series.

Tragedy

At the end of 1972, Clemente had just completed the most satisfying stretch of his long baseball career. The Pittsburgh Pirates won the World Series in 1971 and he was named MVP of the event. He concluded the 1972 season by collecting his long-sought 3,000th hit. He had made public his dream to create a Sports City for disadvantaged youth and had begun fund-raising. His family was healthy and growing. He was 38 years old and, although he intended to resume playing for the Pirates in the spring of 1973, he knew that the end of his baseball career approached. Soon he would devote more time to worthy projects to benefit humanity.

Clemente had much to celebrate on New Years Eve of 1972. But instead of reflecting on his good fortune, he was heavily involved trying to fix others' misfortunes. On December 23, an earthquake had shaken the city of Managua, the capital of Nicaragua. It caused serious damage, and thousands of people lost their homes.

Paid What He Was Worth

For many years, Clemente felt the Pirates underpaid him. He always believed that being a Latino, whose first language was Spanish, held him back in negotiations for a better contract. He eventually reached the point where he was paid in excess of $100,000. That, in his mind, was the deserving salary of a star. Before his death, the Pirates had planned to send him a new contract for the 1973 season calling once again for a six-figure salary.

Clemente's compassion would not allow him to stay idle. As a famous baseball player, his name carried clout. By throwing his energy into the cause, Clemente gained use of an airplane to fly from San Juan to deliver emergency food to people suffering from the earthquake. The shipment included tons of rice, beans, sugar, milk, and meat.

Commitment to Others

Rushing to pull the shipment together, Clemente skipped the New Year's festivities. Friends and family told him he had done enough by organizing the mercy flight and that he should stay home. But Clemente did not feel his mission was complete without distributing the food in Nicaragua. There had been two other supply flights that Clemente organized. He chartered the DC-7 plane for what was scheduled to be the final flight.

He told those close to him that he would quickly return to Puerto Rico. When Clemente's wife, Vera, drove him to the airport, he seemed undecided about

Clemente wanted to deliver food to those affected by the earthquake in Managua, Nicaragua, in 1971.

making the journey. But in the end, he ultimately decided to go.

The plane carrying Clemente and four others took off at 9:20 p.m. Almost immediately, the DC-7 was in trouble. Some suggested it did not have enough speed to take off properly. Others said they heard explosions. There were reports that the plane was overloaded. And it was later revealed that the plane had a list of mechanical problems.

Radio contact was lost. After clearing the runway, the plane lost altitude and plunged directly into the Atlantic Ocean. It was perhaps only a mile off the shore of Puerto Rico.

Shock and Dismay

Word that Clemente was missing spread quickly. The government began an intensive, large-scale search for survivors. A day later, US Navy divers were dispatched to the site. One body—not Clemente's—was dragged from the sea.

At home, Clemente's three sons, then 7, 5, and 4, were asleep before the plane took off. His oldest, Roberto Jr., had chillingly said aloud that this

Haunting Nightmare

When Clemente died in a plane crash, Jose Pagan, his old Pirates teammate who was also from Puerto Rico, said he remembered being on a road-trip flight with Clemente years earlier. Clemente had fallen asleep, but awoke suddenly. He told Pagan he dreamed that he was in a plane crash and that he was the only one who died. Pagan soothed Clemente by saying that he dreamed about being rich, but that had not come true.

plane would crash. He had once again tried to find the plane tickets to hide, but there were no tickets for the charter flight. Vera also had a powerful feeling that something was going to go wrong. While Clemente boarded the flight, she sat in her kitchen and cried.

By midnight, the moment when people shout, "Happy New Year!" and sip champagne, some members of the Puerto Rican and Pirates baseball communities had heard about the crash. Instead of celebrating, they prayed for Clemente, hoping against the facts that he might be found alive. One of the first of Clemente's Pirates teammates to hear about the plane crash was Steve Blass. "My God," was his first thought. "Clemente! He's invincible. He doesn't die. He plays as long as he wants to and then becomes governor of Puerto Rico."[1]

A Friend's Disbelief

Manny Sanguillen, the Pirates' catcher who came from Panama, was a great admirer of Clemente as a player and a man. When he heard that Clemente died in a plane crash, he could not believe it. He immediately went to the beaches of Puerto Rico. After the official search for Clemente's body ended, Sanguillen dove into the waters. Time and again he hurled himself under the waves, desperately trying to find some evidence of his friend. Nothing Sanguillen did could bring Clemente back.

A navy diver inspected debris from the plane that crashed and killed five people, including Clemente, on December 31, 1972.

As the Coast Guard and then the US Navy searched the deep waters, friends, family, baseball fans, and average citizens arrived at the beach and quietly watched the water lap the shore. Pieces of debris turned up, but no bodies. The navy divers touched bottom at 150 feet (46 m), but said the water was very dirty and visibility was limited.

The New Year's holiday turned into a day of mourning. The inauguration of a new governor, Hernandez Colon, had been scheduled for January 1, with accompanying fanfare and more parties. The ceremony was delayed for a day and celebrations were called off. As sadness spread, all anyone could talk about was Roberto Clemente. "The hearts of all of us are in sorrow," Colon said in his inauguration speech.[2]

Orlando Cepeda, another Puerto Rican baseball star who became a Hall of Famer, said that he felt a subdued atmosphere that New Year's Eve even before

Tributes

One person who recognized the special traits of Clemente was Pirates team owner John Galbreath. He was thrilled to have a perennial All-Star and Gold Glove winner roaming his outfield. But he also appreciated the type of honor Clemente brought to his franchise by being a charitable and giving man. "If you have to die," said Galbreath, "how better could your death be exemplified than by being on a mission of mercy? It was so typical of the man."[3]

Bowie Kuhn, the commissioner of baseball, spoke of Clemente's skill on the field and style off of it. "Words seem futile in the face of this tragedy." Kuhn said. "Nor can they possibly do justice to this unique man. Somehow, Roberto transcended superstardom. His marvelous playing skills rank him among the truly elite. And what a wonderfully good man he was! Always concerned about others. He had about him the touch of royalty."[4]

New Puerto Rican governor Hernandez Colon, whose inauguration was overshadowed by Clemente's death, said, "Our youth loses an idol and an example. Our people lose one of their glories."[5]

Spreading Bad News

Many of the Pittsburgh Pirates' team officials and players heard about Clemente's death from the same source. The team's public relations man, Bill Guilfoile, was one of the first to learn of the plane crash, and it was his job to make sure that people knew the truth. He first called General Manager Joe L. Brown, but Brown was so upset he did not properly hang up his phone, making Guilfoile's home telephone impossible to use. In this era before cell phones, Guilfoile had to gather all the loose change he could find in his children's piggy banks and go out into the snowy night to find a pay phone. From there he made the calls delivering the terrible story.

the crash. He heard fewer fireworks than usual, saw fewer people dancing in the street. And then things got worse. "It was quiet and sad," Cepeda said.[6]

The search continued as a day passed, another night, and another day. There was no sign of Roberto Clemente. Hope faded that he could have survived. Now, not even his body could be retrieved. At empty Three Rivers Stadium, the Pirates lighted a simple message on the scoreboard. It read, "Roberto Clemente, 1934–1972."

Vera Clemente, *in black*, stood with her and Roberto's children, *left*, at Roberto's funeral on January 14, 1973, at Hiram Bithorn Stadium in San Juan, Puerto Rico.

CHAPTER 10

Vera Clemente represented her husband when he was enshrined into the Baseball Hall of Fame in 1973.

Aftermath

Denial was the first reaction of those close to Clemente when they heard about his death. No one could quite believe that he was gone. Not his wife nor his children. Not his other relatives. Not his friends. Not the people of Puerto Rico. And not baseball fans in Pittsburgh.

Clemente was just 38 years old. He was still in the prime of his life. An active player, he was due to return to the Pirates' lineup in the spring. Even if he was likely to soon retire from baseball, Clemente had big plans for the rest of his life, such as his Sports City.

The feeling of loss among his young children, who would not have a father, and his wife, who would never marry again, was the keenest. Others missed his friendship and spirit. And still others who viewed him as a great man and a great baseball player felt sorry for the world's loss.

Hall of Fame

Tears were shed, and promises were made. Some pledged to carry out Clemente's dream of creating a Sports City for young people in Puerto Rico. Clemente's long career with the Pirates had produced fabulous statistics that made an election into the Baseball Hall of Fame likely. Under the rules, a player must be retired for five years before his name can be placed on the Hall of Fame ballot.

The Baseball Writers Association of America was in the midst of choosing new members for the Hall of Fame. Approximately 30 writers included Clemente as a write-in candidate. A meeting was held and it was determined that the rules would be waived for Clemente—just as they had been for a dying Lou Gehrig in 1939. The waiting period was eliminated, and Clemente

Roberto Memorabilia

For baseball fans who wish to collect souvenirs of Clemente's playing career, they are easy to find. Items relating to Clemente are available in many forms. These range from postcards to posters, baseball cards to pins, magazines to programs, figurines to pennants, drinking glasses to place mats, photographs to calendars, postal cachets with his picture to solicitation brochures for fund-raising for the Pittsburgh Clemente statue, framed photographs to replicas of the statue that stands next to PNC Park, the Pirates' new stadium. Prices range from a few dollars to many hundreds of dollars.

was considered for Hall of Fame induction immediately. He was quickly selected. On August 6, 1973, Roberto Clemente was inducted into the Hall of Fame. Vera Clemente represented him.

"This is a momentous last triumph," she said, "and if he were here he would dedicate it to the people of Puerto Rico, our people in Pittsburgh, and to all his fans throughout the United States."[1]

Clemente's Premonition

Clemente did not have a death wish, but he thought fatalistically. Many times he spoke in gloomy terms to his wife, saying he did not expect to live long. He did not indicate how he might die as young as 38, but he seemed to have an inner awareness that he would not live to old age. "He was always saying that he was going to die young, very young," Vera Clemente said.[3]

It was far from Clemente's last triumph. During the 1973 season, the Pirates retired his number 21 uniform. That meant that no future Pirates player would ever wear his number. On the field, however, the Pirates suffered greatly from the loss of one of their best players. "It really hurt our ball club," said second baseman Dave Cash. "It hurt the morale of the club. We were stunned when it happened."[2]

When Clemente died, President Richard M. Nixon praised him. He also wrote a personal check for $1,000 to the Nicaraguan relief fund. Funds sprang up in Clemente's name to continue the support for that country.

The Sports City Is Built

Fund-raising continued and a Sports City was constructed in Clemente's name in Carolina, Puerto Rico. The government donated 300 acres (121 ha) of land and $13 million was raised for construction. Among the facilities available for kids were baseball fields, batting cages, a swimming pool, volleyball courts, and a track and field stadium. An estimated 200,000 children visit the sports complex each year. Several children who played on its grounds went on to become major league players, including Ivan Rodriguez,

Roberto Clemente Jr.

The oldest of Clemente's three sons, Roberto Jr., was seven when his father died. While all of the boys were fans of baseball, none reached the majors. Two played professional ball in the minors, however.

As Roberto Jr. grew into adulthood and his baseball hopes were cut short because of knee injuries, he began devoting his life to worthy causes. In Puerto Rico, he became involved in Major League Baseball's RBI program— Reviving Baseball in the Inner Cities. In the 1990s, he worked to create a Roberto Clemente Foundation in Pittsburgh.

Patterning the idea of the Sports City his father had envisioned for Puerto Rico, the foundation was designed to aid the needy and provide educational programs for young people. "I love working with kids," Roberto Jr. said. "It's something you can't put a price on if you have patience and see them come out with self-esteem and self-respect."[4]

Roberto Jr. said there were pressures growing up without a father and in bearing the famous name, which meant he was always in the public eye. He said circumstances made him grow up quickly and mature.

A statue of Roberto Clemente stands outside the Pittsburgh Pirates' ballbark, PNC Park.

Roberto Clemente Award

By definition, the player given the Roberto Clemente Award by Major League Baseball "best exemplifies the game of baseball, sportsmanship, community involvement and the individual's contribution to his team." The award was established in 1971, but starting in 1973 it was named after Clemente.

Winners include: Al Kaline, 1973; Willie Stargell, 1974; Rod Carew, 1977; Ozzie Smith, 1995; Jim Thome, 2002; Edgar Martinez, 2004; Carlos Delgado, 2006; Albert Pujols, 2008; and Derek Jeter, 2009. Martinez and Delgado are the only winners from Puerto Rico.

Rey Sanchez, Ruben Sierra, and Carlos Baerga. Following the Clemente example, those players returned to teach new generations of youngsters.

Vera Clemente, with help from a board of directors, oversees the Sports City's operations. She said if Clemente could see it, he would like what was done in his name. "I think Roberto is very satisfied and happy with what's happening," she said. "After all these years, we're winning the battle."[5]

Many Honors

Within months of Clemente's death, he was posthumously awarded the Congressional Gold Medal. In 1984, he appeared on a US postage stamp. In 2002, he was awarded the Presidential Medal of Freedom, the highest civilian honor in the United States. There is a 10,000-seat indoor

Roberto Clemente Coliseum in San Juan. And a 12,500-seat Roberto Clemente Stadium was built in Carolina for baseball.

In 1994, the Pirates erected a statue of Clemente. It now stands outside PNC Park, the stadium that replaced Three Rivers.

Not long before Clemente died, Major League Baseball had introduced a new award honoring a player combining top-notch play with service to his community. In the third year of its existence, the award's name became the "Roberto Clemente Award." Every year, each of the 30 teams in the majors selects a player as a local winner. A finalist is chosen as the one who best represents the ideals and talents of Roberto Clemente.

During the World Series each year, the award is announced to the world. In this manner, the connection between Roberto Clemente the player and Roberto Clemente the humanitarian is forever linked and reinforced in the minds of baseball fans.

Clemente Legacy

At the beginning of the 2009 Major League Baseball season, 29 percent of the players on the rosters of the 30 teams came from Latin American countries. In Clemente's playing days, those of Hispanic heritage were a much smaller minority. "No question he inspired so many Latin players, especially players from the Caribbean area, to work hard and to reach the major leagues," said Jaime Jarrin, who has broadcast Los Angeles Dodgers games in Spanish for 50 years. "He knew that he had the responsibility of opening the doors for other players."[6]

Neil Walker

Tom Walker was playing winter ball in Puerto Rico in 1972 when the earthquake hit Nicaragua. Along with some other players, he helped Clemente load the airplane with supplies to help the victims. But when Walker and the others asked to join Clemente on the trip, Clemente said no. He did not want them to miss their New Year's Eve party. "He saved my life by not letting me get on that plane," Walker said.[8] Thirty-seven years later, in 2009, Tom's son Neil Walker debuted for the Pirates. He played in 110 games in 2010 and batted .296 with 66 RBIs.

In 1997, as a tribute to Jackie Robinson, baseball retired the number 42 for every major league team. In 2005, a movement began to convince baseball to make the same gesture for Clemente. Those who believe in his legend and the way he eased the path for Latin American players seek to have his number 21 retired by all teams too.

"Roberto Clemente," said Fernando Mateo, president of Hispanics Across America, "was our true national hero in terms of baseball, the way he lived his life, the way he died to save others."[7]

Roberto Clemente is remembered as a national hero in Puerto Rico and a Latin American trailblazer in Major League Baseball.

1934

Roberto Clemente is born in Carolina, Puerto Rico.

1942

Clemente plays on a local slow-pitch softball team, his first organized team.

1948

Clemente joins a more competitive little league-level local softball team.

1952

Clemente attends a Brooklyn Dodgers tryout camp in Puerto Rico on November 6 and makes an impression, but no deal is offered.

1952–1953

Clemente plays for the Crabbers.

1954

Clemente signs to play with the Brooklyn Dodgers organization on February 19. He receives a $10,000 bonus and a $5,000 salary.

1950

Clemente switches to hardball and plays on his first local baseball team.

1950–1951

Clemente emerges as a baseball and track and field star at Vizcarrondo High School.

1952

Clemente is signed by the Santurce Crabbers, a local professional team, on October 9 after owner Pedrin Zorrilla sees him play.

1954

Because the Dodgers fail to protect him properly, the Pittsburgh Pirates draft Clemente on November 22.

1955

Clemente makes his major league debut against the Dodgers on April 17.

1956

For the first time, Clemente bats over .300 when he hits .311.

1960

Clemente is chosen for the National League All-Star team for the first of 12 times.

1960

Clemente is the starting right fielder on the Pirates' World Series championship team.

1961

Clemente wins the first of 12 Gold Glove Awards. He hits .351 to claim the first of four batting titles.

1967

Clemente captures his fourth batting title with a .357 average.

1971

Clemente is a leader on the Pirates' World Series championship team and is named MVP of the World Series in October.

1972

A double marks Clemente's milestone 3,000th hit against the New York Mets on September 30.

1964

Clemente hits .339 for his second batting title and leads the National League with 211 hits.

1965

Clemente wins his third batting title with a .329 mark.

1966

Clemente wins the National League Most Valuable Player Award.

1972

Clemente is killed in a plane crash while trying to fulfill a charitable mission to deliver emergency supplies to earthquake-stricken Nicaragua on December 31.

1973

Clemente is elected to the Baseball Hall of Fame on March 20.

1974

The Roberto Clemente Sports City is created.

ESSENTIAL FACTS

DATE OF BIRTH

August 18, 1934

PLACE OF BIRTH

Carolina, Puerto Rico

DATE OF DEATH

December 31, 1972

PLACE OF DEATH

San Juan, Puerto Rico

PARENTS

Luisa Walker and Melchor Clemente

EDUCATION

Vizcarrondo High School

MARRIAGE

Vera (November 14, 1964)

CHILDREN

Roberto Jr., Enrique, Luis

CAREER HIGHLIGHTS

Roberto Clemente was a Major League Baseball Hall of Fame outfielder. He spent 18 seasons with the Pittsburgh Pirates with a lifetime batting average of .317. The winner of the 1966 Most Valuable Player Award, Clemente was also a 12-time National League All-Star, won 12 Gold Glove Awards for his fielding, and won four batting titles. He played on the 1960 and 1971 Pirates World Series championship teams and won the Most Valuable Player Award in the 1971 World Series.

SOCIAL CONTRIBUTIONS

Clemente was regarded as a pioneer Latin American baseball star who spoke out against discrimination committed against dark-skinned players and players of Hispanic heritage. His pride in his Latino heritage and accomplishments made him a spokesman for all Latino players. He distinguished himself by volunteering time and effort to charitable work in Pittsburgh and Puerto Rico.

CONFLICTS

Clemente was sometimes misunderstood because Spanish was his first language and because he complained often about injuries. Decades after his death, Clemente is still revered by the baseball world and particularly by those of Hispanic background.

QUOTE

"This is something that from the first day, I said to myself: 'I am the minority group. I am from the poor people. I represent the poor people. I represent the common people of America. So I am going to be treated as a human being.'"
—*Roberto Clemente*

GLOSSARY

All-Star

A player selected for the All-Star team represents the league he plays in (either American or National) during an annual exhibition baseball game held each July.

batting title

Over the course of a season, the player who bats for the highest percentage, based on number of hits compared to the number of at-bats.

bonus

A one-time payment made to a baseball prospect when he signs with a club, separate from his regular annual salary.

color barrier

For more than 60 years, until 1947, Major League Baseball discriminated against players with dark skin, refusing to let them compete at the highest level of professional baseball.

discrimination

Unfair treatment of people based on prejudice.

exhibition game

A game in which the teams play to develop skills and promote the sport rather than for a competitive advantage.

general manager

A managerial position within a baseball team's organization. The general manager signs new players, makes trades, and negotiates contracts.

Hispanic

Relating to people who are of Spanish or Latin American descent. Countries in the Caribbean, as well as Central and South America, that were once part of the Spanish empire.

hits
When a batter safely reaches base without being walked or a fielder committing an error.

manager
The field boss of a baseball team, equal to the head coach in basketball and football.

pioneer
A person who leads all others into new areas of thought or development.

postal cachet
An official seal on a document, such as a letter.

racism
The unfair treatment of people based on race.

retired number
A team honors a great player by not allowing any future players to wear the same jersey number.

rookie
A first-year player in Major League Baseball.

scout
A baseball representative who looks for talented athletes to play for a team.

solicitation
The act of trying to get somebody to do something.

winter ball
During the Major League Baseball off-season, many players join teams in warmer locations such as Puerto Rico.

ADDITIONAL RESOURCES

SELECTED BIBLIOGRAPHY

Maraniss, David. *Clemente: The Passion and Grace of Baseball's Last Hero*. New York: Simon & Schuster, 2006. Print.

Markusen, Bruce. *Roberto Clemente: The Great One*. Champaign, IL: Sports Publishing LLC, 1998. Print.

National Baseball Hall of Fame Library Archives Roberto Clemente File, Cooperstown, New York. Print.

O'Brien, Jim. *Remember Roberto*. Pittsburgh, PA: Geyer Printing Company, Inc., 1994. Print.

United Press International Staff. *Roberto Clemente*. New York: Tempo Books, 1973. Print.

FURTHER READINGS

Vecsey, George. *Baseball: A History of America's Favorite Game*. New York: Modern Library, 2008. Print.

Walker, Paul Robert. *Pride of Puerto Rico: The Life of Roberto Clemente*. San Diego, CA: Harcourt Brace Jovanovich Pub., 1991. Print.

Winter, Jonah. *Roberto Clemente: Pride of the Pittsburgh Pirates*. New York: Atheneum Books for Young Readers, 2005. Print.

WEB LINKS

To learn more about Roberto Clemente, visit ABDO Publishing Company online at **www.abdopublishing.com**.
Web sites about Clemente are featured on our Book Links page. These links are routinely monitored and updated to provide the most current information available.

PLACES TO VISIT

National Baseball Hall of Fame
25 Main Street, Cooperstown, New York, 13326
1-888-HALL-OF-FAME
www.baseballhalloffame.org
Roberto Clemente was elected as a member of the National Baseball Hall of Fame soon after his death. The museum routinely rotates exhibits, but a plaque commemorating his selection is always on display.

PNC Park
115 Federal Street, Pittsburgh, Pennsylvania, 15212
412-323-5000
www.pittsburgh.pirates.mlb.com
The Pittsburgh Pirates have honored Roberto Clemente in many ways. Among them are a statue of Clemente that stands near the Roberto Clemente Bridge, which formerly was called the Sixth Street Bridge.

Roberto Clemente Sports City
802 Iturregui Avenue, Carolina, Puerto Rico, 00982
787-750-2100
www.rcsc21.com/index_en.php
After his death, Roberto Clemente was honored in his hometown with the construction of two stadiums. Professional teams use the main Roberto Clemente Stadium. A second Roberto Clemente Stadium is part of the Ciudad Deportiva Roberto Clemente, also known as the Roberto Clemente Sports City. Amateur teams play there.

CHAPTER 1. Chasing 3,000 Hits

1. Bruce Markusen. *Roberto Clemente: The Great One*. Champaign, IL: Sports Publishing LLC, 1998. Print. 299.

2. Jim O'Brien. *Remember Roberto*. Pittsburgh, PA: Geyer Printing Company, 1994. Print. 108.

3. "Clemente Notches No. 3,000, Officially." *New York Times*. 1 Oct. 1972. Print. S1.

4. Ira Miller, et al. *Roberto Clemente*. New York: Tempo Books, 1973. Print. 55.

5. Bruce Markusen. *Roberto Clemente: The Great One*. Champaign, IL: Sports Publishing LLC, 1998. Print. 298.

CHAPTER 2. Early Life

1. Bruce Markusen. *Roberto Clemente: The Great One*. Champaign, IL: Sports Publishing LLC, 1998. Print. 3.

2. Ira Miller, et al. *Roberto Clemente*. New York: Tempo Books, 1973. Print. 10.

3. Ibid. 12.

4. David Maraniss. *Clemente: The Passion and Grace of Baseball's Last Hero*. New York: Simon & Schuster, 2006. Print. 21.

5. Ira Miller, et al. *Roberto Clemente*. New York: Tempo Books, 1973. Print. 14.

6. Bruce Markusen. *Roberto Clemente: The Great One*. Champaign, IL: Sports Publishing LLC, 1998. Print. 5.

7. David Maraniss. *Clemente: The Passion and Grace of Baseball's Last Hero*. New York: Simon & Schuster, 2006. Print. 26.

CHAPTER 3. Being Discovered

1. David Maraniss. *Clemente: The Passion and Grace of Baseball's Last Hero*. New York: Simon & Schuster, 2006. Print. 26.

2. Ibid. 27.

3. Bruce Markusen. *Roberto Clemente: The Great One*. Champaign, IL: Sports Publishing LLC, 1998. Print. 13.

4. Ira Miller, et al. *Roberto Clemente*. New York: Tempo Books, 1973. Print. 14–15.

5. Bruce Markusen. *Roberto Clemente: The Great One.* Champaign, IL: Sports Publishing LLC, 1998. Print. 16.

CHAPTER 4. Becoming a Pirate

1. Bruce Markusen. *Roberto Clemente: The Great One.* Champaign, IL: Sports Publishing LLC, 1998. Print. 52.

2. Don Hall. "Clarkson Gave Roberto An Early Boost." *Valley News-Dispatch* (Pennsylvania). National Baseball Hall of Fame Library Archives, date cut off. Print.

3. Bruce Markusen. *Roberto Clemente: The Great One.* Champaign, IL: Sports Publishing LLC, 1998. Print. 52.

CHAPTER 5. Becoming a Star

1. John Carroll. "Basket Catch Enables Clemente to Hold Ball." *Simpson's Leader-Times.* 7 May 1957. Print. 10.

2. David Maraniss. *The Passion and Grace of Baseball's Last Hero.* New York: Simon & Schuster, 2006. Print. 70.

3. Les Biederman. "Drafted For $4000, Clemente Becomes Bucs' Top Bargain." *Pittsburgh Press.* 10 Apr. 1958. Print. n. pag.

4. Jim O'Brien. *Remember Roberto.* Pittsburgh, PA: Greyer Printing Company, Inc., 1994. Print. 128–129.

5. Ira Miller, et al. *Roberto Clemente.* New York: Tempo Books, 1973. Print. 25.

6. Bruce Markusen. *Roberto Clemente: The Great One.* Champaign, IL: Sports Publishing LLC, 1998. Print. 80.

CHAPTER 6. Hispanic Pride

1. Robert Heuer. "Clemente's Legacy for Latin Ballplayers." *New York Times.* 2 Jan. 1983. Print. S2.

2. Bill Christine. "Sports Writers Batting .000 With Clemente." *Pittsburgh Press.* 2 Apr. 1969. Print. n. pag.

3. Bruce Markusen. *Roberto Clemente: The Great One.* Champaign, IL: Sports Publishing LLC, 1998. Print. 47.

4. Rob Ruck. "Remembering Roberto Clemente." *Pittsburgh Magazine.* Dec. 1992. Print. n. pag.

5. Robert Heuer. "Clemente's Legacy for Latin Ballplayers." *New York Times.* 2 Jan. 1983. Print. S2.

6. Bruce Markusen. *Roberto Clemente: The Great One.* Champaign, IL: Sports Publishing LLC, 1998. Print. 176.

7. David Maraniss. *Clemente: The Passion and Grace of Baseball's Last Hero.* New York: Simon & Schuster, 2006. Print. 71.

CHAPTER 7. The Biggest Stage

1. Bruce Markusen. *Roberto Clemente: The Great One.* Champaign, IL: Sports Publishing LLC, 1998. Print. 101.

2. Jim O'Brien. *Maz And The '60 Bucs.* Pittsburgh, PA: Geyer Printing Company, Inc., 1993. Print. 256.

3. Jim O'Brien. *Remember Roberto.* Pittsburgh, PA: Geyer Printing Company, Inc., 1994. Print. 314.

4. Ibid.

5. George Diaz. "Roberto Clemente: A Vocal Leader For Equality." *Orlando Sentinel.* Puerto Rico Herald, 31 Mar. 2002. Web. 4 Oct. 2010.

6. Ibid.

7. "Murtaugh, Williams: Roberto Was the Greatest." *Tri-City Herald.* 2 Jan. 1972. Print. 18.

8. "Roberto Clemente Quotes." *Baseball Almanac.* Baseball Almanac, *2005.* Web. 1 Apr. 2010.

CHAPTER 8. The Great One

1. Rob Ruck. "Remembering Roberto." *Pittsburgh Magazine.* Dec. 1992. Print. n. pag.

2. Peter C. Bjarkman. *Baseball with a Latin Beat: A History of the Latin American Game.* Jefferson, NC: McFarland, 1994. Print. 76.

3. Ira Miller, et al. *Roberto Clemente.* New York: Tempo Books, 1973. Print. 37.

4. "Roberto Clemente Night." *Pittsburgh Pirates Game Program.* 24 July 1970. Print. n. pag.

5. Ira Miller, et al. *Roberto Clemente.* New York: Tempo Books, 1973. Print. 52–53.

CHAPTER 9. Tragedy

1. David Maraniss. *Clemente: The Passion and Grace of Baseball's Last Hero.* New York: Simon & Schuster, 2006. Print. 335.

2. "U.S. Divers Join Clemente Search." *The Free Lance-Star.* 3 Jan. 1972. Print. 8.

3. "He Was a Friend—Galbreath." *The Pittsburgh Press.* 2 Jan. 1973. Print. 25.

4. Ibid.

5. Hamilton Bims. "Roberto Clemente: Sad End for a Troubled Man." *Ebony.* March 1973. Print. 60.

6. David Maraniss. *Clemente: The Passion and Grace of Baseball's Last Hero.* New York: Simon & Schuster, 2006. Print. 333.

CHAPTER 10. Aftermath

1. Bruce Markusen. *Roberto Clemente: The Great One.* Champaign, IL: Sports Publishing LLC, 1998. Print. 327.

2. Ibid. 330.

3. Ibid. 314.

4. Claire Smith. "Clemente's Oldest Son the Keeper of the Flame." *New York Times.* 10 Jan. 1994. Print. C2.

5. Kevin Baxter. "Clemente's legacy." *Miami Herald.* Puerto Rico Herald, 31 Dec. 2002. Web. 4 Oct. 2010.

6. Ibid.

7. Shelly Anderson. "Clemente crusade: Group wants Major-League teams to retire Pirates' great's No. 21." *post-gazette.com.* Pittsburgh Post-Gazette, 31 Aug. 2005. Web. 4 Oct. 2010.

8. "Walker Thanks Clemente for Saving Father's Life." *93.7 The Fan.* CBS Radio, 3 Sept. 2010. Web. 20 Oct. 2010.

INDEX

ABOUT THE AUTHOR

Lew Freedman is a longtime sportswriter and the author of 42 books, mostly about sports and Alaska. A veteran sports journalist, he has won more than 250 awards writing for the *Anchorage Daily News*, *Chicago Tribune*, and other newspapers. He has a bachelor's degree in journalism from Boston University and a master of liberal arts degree, with an emphasis in intercultural communication, from Alaska Pacific University. He and his wife live in the Chicago area.

PHOTO CREDITS